D0847848

Columbia University

Contributions to Education

Teachers College Series

No. 472

AMS PRESS
NEW YORK

GENERALIZATION IN SPELLING

A STUDY OF VARIOUS BASES OF
GENERALIZATION IN TEACHING SPELLING

BY

INA CRAIG SARTORIUS, Ph.D.

TEACHERS COLLEGE, COLUMBIA UNIVERSITY
CONTRIBUTIONS TO EDUCATION, No. 472

*Published with the approval of
Professor Arthur I. Gates, Sponsor*

BUREAU OF PUBLICATIONS
Teachers College, Columbia University
NEW YORK CITY
1931

Library of Congress Cataloging in Publication Data

Sartorius, Ina (Craig) 1892–
  Generalization in spelling.

  Reprint of the 1931 ed., issued in series: Teachers
College, Columbia University. Contributions to
education, no. 472.
  Presented also as author's thesis, Columbia.
  Bibliography: p.
  1. English language—Orthography and spelling.
I. Title. II. Series: Columbia University.
Teachers College. Contributions to education, no. 472.
LB1574.S3 1972   372.6'32   76-177229
ISBN 0-404-55472-5

Reprinted by Special Arrangement with Teachers
College Press, New York, New York

From the edition of 1931, New York
First AMS edition published in 1972
Manufactured in the United States

AMS PRESS, INC.
NEW YORK, N. Y.   10003

ACKNOWLEDGMENTS

I wish to express my sincere gratitude to the Chairman and sponsor of my dissertation committee, Professor Arthur I. Gates. His guidance throughout the entire study has made this dissertation possible.

To Professors Rollo G. Reynolds and Edwin H. Reeder I am most grateful for advice and encouragement. Especially to Professor Reynolds do I wish to express my thanks for helpful and stimulating suggestions.

Miss Marion Glass, assistant to Professor Reynolds, has devoted many hours to wearying and monotonous statistical computations which have made it possible to complete this study.

I. C. S.

CONTENTS

TABLES

GENERALIZATION IN SPELLING

∴

CHAPTER I

THE PROBLEM OF GENERALIZATION

OPINIONS

In the teaching of English spelling two fairly distinct points of view have been advanced with reference to the value of generalization. Some authorities place practically all the emphasis upon the acquisition of specific bonds, while others at present are beginning to find evidence to show that there is some basis for building more general bonds.

Until recently the most widely accepted point of view in the United States was that of Ernest Horn. That he once had little confidence in the possibility of generalization, is indicated by such statements as these [7][1]: "Rules cannot replace direct instruction in spelling, even in the case of words covered by them." . . . "Most of the articles dealing with the subject [spelling rules] contain a peculiar fallacy, namely, that by discovering what words are covered by a given rule, one may discover the efficiency of teaching that rule. As a matter of fact, one must show in addition to the above that the rule can be easily taught, that it will be remembered, and that it will function in the stress of actual spelling. Evidence seems to cast a doubt on all three of these assumptions. . . ." "There has been an unfortunate assumption in some quarters that an apparently slight change in the form of a word constitutes no new spelling difficulty. There has also been a tendency to guess whether a given derivation constituted a special problem. Investigations have shown that derivations are practically always more difficult to spell than the forms upon which they are built." Near the conclusion of this comprehensive survey of scientific investigations, he made the following statement: "Attention should be called to the fact

[1] Numerals inclosed in brackets refer to items listed in the Bibliography, page 58.

1

that the evidence as to the most economical method of teaching spelling is not complete."

In more recent articles Horn [9] grants that there may be transfer due to the influence of past experience, but he shows that such transfer is not necessarily always desirable in learning new words. He says: "Attention was called to the possibility that when a child attempts to spell a word for the first time he may be led into error by the fact that the individual sounds in the word have been spelled in a variety of ways in other words which the child has already learned to spell. It was shown that these various spellings of individual sounds can be combined in an enormous number of ways to make the sounds of the word as a whole. The word *circumference* was used as an illustration. The sound in this word can be spelled in 396,900,000 ways by using the spellings of identical or similar sounds in words likely to be known to a sixth grade child. . . ." "It seems probable that these misspellings are caused, at least in part, by transfers from spellings of identical or similar sounds in words which the student knows (or thinks he knows) how to spell. . . ." In the same article he also says: "In teaching spelling, the chief dependence must be placed on learning each word as an individual problem. The more one studies the problems created by the unphonetic character of English spelling, the more he must marvel at the ease and rapidity with which many students learn to spell." He tells us also that "the most helpful principles in spelling are those which apply to adding prefixes and suffixes, to making contractions, and to indicating possession. Even these principles should reïnforce, rather than supplant, instruction on the most important words to which they apply."

In his later writing, Horn [8] comments on the possibilities of generalization as follows: "We have long been taught that learning is facilitated, and remembrance made more certain by utilizing meaningful associations. It is not surprising, therefore, that we have with us always one or more varieties of plans for rationalizing spelling and reading. Learning to spell four thousand different words seems a large task if each word must be learned as an individual task. . . ." "For while the unphonetic character of the English language constitutes a real obstacle to successful rationalization, it is not necessarily an insurmountable one. But the degree to which this obstacle may be surmounted by phonic training, what kind of phonic training is best, and how or when it should be given . . . these are questions for which, at present, there are no answers upon which investigators in reading agree."

That there is some basis for the acquisition of more general bonds is the point of view held by such men as Thorndike and Gates. We quote from Thorndike [13], "The leading expert in this field [English spelling] Ernest Horn, relies almost entirely on the learning of the spelling of each word by itself, having almost no confidence in generalization of any kind in this field. We may agree with him in his skepticism concerning the value of the ordinary rules and similarities as commonly taught and still hope that a more fundamental analysis will indicate certain combinations of generalization and one-by-one learning as superior to the latter alone. For example, the generalizations 'oa is very common, ao is very rare, ea is very common, ae is very rare, ee is very common, aa is very rare' seem worth the minute or two it takes to make them. Probably every child above the imbecile level has a more or less general habit of expressing the sound at the end of a plural word by s rather than z and profits by having it. Wholesale acceptance or rejection of any procedure is risky as a method of teaching. It is often necessary to extend the analysis to each case."

Thorndike and Gates [12] tell us that "the spread of training is genuine even if small in magnitude."

Breed [2] refers to an experimental study by C. P. Archer[1] as evidence to corroborate his own conclusion that "the ability to spell certain words enables one to master more easily the spelling of certain other words; that is, that spelling ability, in some instances, has general value. Experimental studies of the transfer of training would lead one to infer that transference of training from one word to another is possible when the words have similar difficulties or identical elements, and since this theory is supported by experimentation with spelling material, phonetic grouping of words must be regarded as more scientific than random grouping."

A careful analysis of spelling textbooks is discussed in Chapter

[1] A study entitled, "Transfer of Training in Spelling," in the *Elementary English Review*, V (1928), pp. 55-61.

IV. These textbooks can be placed on a curve of distribution on the basis of their use of definitions or rules, which is unquestionably one form of generalization. Table VI, page 28, shows that both the Brown-Burdick and the Horn-Ashbaugh spellers are at one end of the scale, using no rules, while the Thorndike-Wohlfarth and the McCall-Houser spellers each use forty-eight generalized statements, the maximum number in any speller studied. The Trabue-Stevens speller contains thirty-nine generalized statements and the words in the daily lessons are grouped in phonic families. The Smith-Bagley speller has thirty-three generalized statements and makes extensive use of phonetic grouping. This table shows that the question of how much children can be aided in making generalizations by use of rules is still unanswered since our leading authorities differ so widely on this particular point when writing their textbooks.

RESEARCH

The opinions discussed in the foregoing paragraphs are, of course, the points of view of men who base their conclusions upon scientific investigation. The following paragraphs are devoted to excerpts from rather recent research in the field of spelling. The evidence gathered in these later investigations points toward the fact that generalization in spelling does take place.

Wagner [16] in the summary of his experimental study in 1912 wrote as follows: "Grouping words into lessons according to spelling difficulty is better than the ordinary plan of spelling lessons. It secures better daily lessons, better final results, and greater steadiness or constancy of correct spelling. . . ." "The study of words arranged into groups according to similarity in spelling difficulty is 20 per cent better than the usual non-grouping method of arrangement and study."

Tidyman and Johnson [15] in an experiment using eighty words that present certain difficulties for fifth grade children conclude that "grouping words of similar difficulty together in spelling is a significant factor, and that grouping words for study secures approximately ten per cent better results than the study of words in a chance order. The superiority of the grouping method is shown not only in immediate learning, but also in the pupils' ability to spell the words after an interval of twelve weeks. The results of this experiment confirm in a remarkable manner the conclusions of Dr. Wagner in his *Experimental Study of Grouping by Similarity in the Teaching of Spelling*, for he concluded that the rate of improvement of the class using the grouping method was 1.1 times as great as the class not using the grouping method."

Archer [1] writes that "evidence leads us to see that transfer does take place from one word to another, sometimes resulting in an increase of the ability to spell the transfer form and sometimes to interfere with the correct spelling of the unstudied form." This study is among the best in regard to presenting evidence relating to the use of rules and the problem of grouping words in the teaching of spelling.

Carroll [3] concluded from his experiment with bright and dull children that the bright did generalize more than the dull and that generalization was both negative and positive. In an unpublished dissertation [17] Watson states that "the spelling of any word is never an isolated function; it is likely to be affected either adversely or favorably by the readiness and potency of neural bonds formed in previous experiences with somewhat similar words."

Gates and Chase [5] in their work with the deaf place emphasis upon the visual appearance of the word, but feel that generalization through the use of spelling rules helps. We quote them as follows: "The success of the deaf indicates that much may be gained by establishing better habits of visual study of words in learning to spell and then of exercising until firmly mastered the habit of writing the word. Studies to be reported indicate that elementary school pupils write or articulate the spelling only after recalling the letters by translation of sounds to letters or by visualization of letters or by both combined. Since English is so unphonetic, the most reliable device for determining which of the many genuine sound-to-letters translations is the correct one is to be able to recall some impression of the visual appearance of the word. This, I believe, is the method adopted by the deaf . . . with excellent results as we have seen. While the use of spelling rules has largely fallen into disrepute there are theoretical reasons and some experimental evidence tending to show that when used as one of the means of emphasizing the visible similarities and differences among groups of like and unlike word forms they may be fruitfully employed to improve word-perceptive habits and, consequently, spelling ability."

SUMMARY

Certainly the foregoing quotations leave the question of transfer in spelling in a state of apparent confusion. The lines of endeavor represented are varied and the opinions of the writers have developed out of widely differing experiences.

There is need for further research and analysis in practically every aspect of the teaching of spelling. The importance of more comprehensive analysis is clearly indicated by such quotations as the following.

Thorndike [13] says: "Spelling offers another interesting illustration of the need for more penetrating analysis. There is evidence to show that much of the learning and relearning or prevention of forgetting of spelling comes as a by-product of reading. Some individuals, including many of the better spellers, obtain during ordinary reading impressions which leave after-effects adequate to aid in spelling. A method of teaching spelling which, other things being equal, improved ability to perceive words during reading in a way beneficial to later spelling would be highly advantageous. Indeed its influence in this direction might far outweigh its influence in the day-by-day learning of the four or six hundred words assigned for study each year."

Tidyman [14] says: "The formation of rules should be based upon a comparative study of words. In observing the similar changes which words undergo in the formation of plurals, derivatives, and the like, the child may be led to see or may even discover for himself the principles of spelling involved. Thus, generalization . . . that is, rules . . . appear as a natural outcome of the intelligent observation of words, rather than as arbitrary statements.

"The child should be taught the uses of rules as means of correcting errors, aiding the memory and acquiring the spelling of new words. We should bear in mind, however, that spelling by rule does not take the place of a free automatic use of words."

Pryor and Pittman [11] quote the following sentence from Cook, O'Shea and Suzzallo: "It is more economical to spend the time needed to fix the habit of using the rules in the learning of spelling words."

THE PROBLEM

Many of the problems to be solved in connection with spelling clearly indicate the need of a careful analysis of the words themselves, whether used in classroom teaching or in experimentation to determine classroom procedure. This study, therefore, has been devoted to such an analysis of a carefully chosen list of words. The problem is stated in the following outline:

1. To set up a scheme by which a complete visual analysis of the word list can be made, so that it will be possible to tell how common *oa* really is, how rare is *ao*, how common *ea*, how rare *ae*, etc., as Thorndike [13] suggests.
2. To determine at each grade level the frequency of the words containing these visual elements.
3. To make a phonetic analysis of the word list, such as has been done partially with some reading vocabularies.
4. To determine at each grade level the frequency of these phonograms.
5. To study the correct pronunciation of these phonograms with the aid of a standard dictionary in order to determine the number of ways a given visual element may be pronounced.
6. To get an accurate count of the rules now found in current spellers, and then analyze the list of words with reference to the most commonly accepted rules.
7. To determine exactly the grade placement of all words governed by the most commonly accepted rules.
8. To determine the frequency by grades of the word elements with relation to the common errors actually made by children writing these words.

It is hoped that such an analysis will indicate certain lines of procedure which may be of real value to textbook writers and to those engaged in further research on such questions as the following:

1. Shall a given rule be taught?
2. Shall a given rule be introduced first at the grade level

where the first word governed by that rule appears or at the grade level where there is the greatest frequency of use?

3. Granted a rule is worth teaching, at what grade level shall it be taught to insure the least forgetting?

4. Where will the rule function best in the stress of actual spelling?

5. Do derivatives constitute a new spelling difficulty? Is it probable that this depends upon the order in which the various forms are given? What is the relative frequency of different kinds of derivatives?

6. If, as Horn [9] says, "the most helpful principles in spelling are those which apply to adding prefixes and suffixes, to making contractions, and to indicating possession," what bases for explaining and utilizing this fact appear in the body of most commonly taught words?

7. How can grouping of words make for positive transfer and lessen negative transfer? How can exceptions to the rule be located and handled?

8. Can homonyms be grouped together?

9. If, as Archer [1] says, "Children will do their own generalizing anyway," what influence is the frequency of different "common factors" in a typical spelling list likely to have? What helpful and what misleading generalizations is the unguided learner likely to make?

10. From studies of frequencies of appearance and grade distribution of common visual and phonetic elements, words covered by rules or exceptions to rules, words susceptible to particular misspelling by analogy and the like, what suggestions may be made for giving the pupils' inevitable tendency to generalize the best possible guidance?

CHAPTER II

WORD LIST USED IN THIS STUDY

The present investigation was designed to reveal various possible bases of generalization found in the listed words commonly taught in the spelling courses and written by children in school work in the United States. In order to make the results of greatest possible use at the present time, it became necessary to select a word list most adequate for the purpose. Here were involved two problems: (1) determining the number of words to include in the list, and (2) selecting the words most useful for the purposes of the study.

A survey of spelling books reveals considerable variation in the number of words taught. For example, a study of sixteen textbooks in common use at the present time shows a range in the word list from 3,732 to 5,370 words. In many of these books, however, a considerable number of words are given in supplementary lists, and are probably studied only by a small proportion of the most able students. It appears that in general the majority of students encounter about 4,000 words in the actual spelling lessons undertaken in the first eight grades. Studies by Horn have shown, furthermore, that 4,000 words will comprise approximately 98 per cent of the running words found in the writing of adults. In all probability, the writing of children in the school grades would show a smaller number of words to comprise 98 per cent of their compositions. Since 4,000 words represent approximately 98 per cent of the words used with any degree of frequency by both children and adults, and since the typical speller provides instruction in approximately 4,000 words for the average child in the first eight grades, it was decided that the list to use for this study should consist of approximately 4,000 words. The list as finally selected includes, to be exact, 4,065 words. These words are believed to represent those most frequently taught to children and also those most frequently used in the writing of children and adults.

9

Having decided that the list should comprise approximately 4,000 words, it next became necessary to determine what particular words should be used in the study. These words might have been selected by one of two methods: (1) selecting the words which appear with the greatest frequency in the studies of the writing, reading, and speaking of adults, or (2) selecting the words which appear most frequently in the most widely used courses in spelling. The first type of approach would presumably give those words which most deserve to be studied, whereas the second approach would give those words which actually are most frequently taught in the schools of America.

Shortly before this study was undertaken, an investigation of spelling words had been made by Dr. Arthur I. Gates and Mr. Frederick B. Graham. These investigators drew up a list in which the two preceding criteria were combined. The list was composed of all the words in the Ayres-Buckingham Spelling List, the first 5,000 words in the Horn Basic Vocabulary, the 2,916 word-forms in the Gates Primary Reading List, and all derived as well as basal forms of the first 4,000 words in the Thorndike Word List. These data were combined with all the words listed in the following seven spellers, which are believed to be so widely used in this country that they would represent the words studied in school by a very large proportion of children.

1. Horn-Ashbaugh Fundamentals of Spelling
2. Lippincott's New Horn-Ashbaugh Speller
3. The New York City List
4. Jones' Complete Course in Spelling
5. The McCall Speller
6. Smith-Bagley Mastery Speller
7. Breed-French Speller

Since the 4,065 words selected represent those most commonly appearing in widely used spelling textbooks and those which appear with the greatest frequency in the best-known studies of children's usage, it is believed that they represent approximately the words most commonly taught in the first eight grades in this country and also those most commonly used by the children in these grades. It should be pointed out in this connection that in the schools in which no spelling textbook is used the words are usually selected from those of highest frequency in such studies of word usages as were incorporated. This being the case, the studies of phonetic and visual elements, of conformities and exceptions to rules, and of the frequencies with which various common errors are likely to be made may be said to represent certain bases of generalization found in the common spelling vocabulary of American children.

After the words were selected, they were grouped into grade lists. This was desirable, since, if a person were interested, for example, in using one of the rules which is found to be applicable to a great many words with relatively few exceptions, it would be of value to know the grade distribution of the words which might be used in connection with the rule. For example, if among the words falling under a rule very few are taught in Grades 2 and 3 and a very large number are taught in Grade 4, it might be desirable not to attempt to introduce the generalizations based on this rule until the fourth grade. Furthermore, if one were attempting to organize material to illustrate the rule, it would be advantageous to be able easily to select those words conforming to the rule which appear in any particular grade.

In assigning words to grades the following method was utilized. First, the proportion of the total number of words assigned to each of several grades in the textbooks above enumerated was determined. The assignments made for the purposes of this study represent approximately the average proportions found by combining the practices of these several books. Having determined these proportions, the words were assigned by consolidating the results, first, of several studies, such as the well-known Ayres-Buckingham and Horn-Ashbaugh data on the difficulty of words, and, second, the grade placements of the words found in the textbooks above enumerated. The final result, consequently, represents again the average or typical practice. That is to say, each word is placed in that grade in which it is probably most commonly taught in the schools of the country. The number of words assigned to each grade is indicated in Table I.

It should, of course, be understood that the number of words selected for the study, the number of words assigned to the several grades, and the grade placements of the particular words used are not presented as being ideal. They are merely offered as representing approximately the most common practice in the

TABLE I

TOTAL NUMBER OF WORDS IN EACH GRADE

Grade	Words	Grade	Words
Grade 2A	192	Grade 6A	320
Grade 2B	192	Grade 6B	320
Grade 3A	240	Grade 7A	320
Grade 3B	256	Grade 7B	320
Grade 4A	312	Grade 8A	320
Grade 4B	312	Grade 8B	320
Grade 5A	320		
Grade 5B	321	Total	4,065

country. The analyses of the basis of generalization may therefore be said to give an indication of the possibilities which exist in the spelling vocabularies most widely used at the present time.

CHAPTER III

POSSIBILITIES OF PHONETIC AND VISUAL GENERALIZATION

RESULTS OF INVESTIGATIONS AND OPINIONS OF EXPERTS

In the report of a recent study made by Carroll [3] there was presented evidence that children use phonetic translation which is the outcome of generalization in its most common form. Carroll also found that bright children generalize phonetically more than do dull children. He further concluded, in agreement with Horn and Archer, that the generalization may be negative as well as positive.

Many writers of modern popular textbooks in spelling recommend or make use of either phonetic or visual elements or both when they set up the daily lessons to be taught. They group together in daily or weekly lessons words of phonetic families or words having visual similarities. Breed [2] specifically says that "two points should be observed in organizing" lesson units, namely, "1. Words that are phonetically and orthographically similar should appear together. 2. Homonyms should appear together." He bases these conclusions on the experiments of Tidyman [14], Wagner [16], and H. C. Pearson.[1] The *Breed-French Speller* is organized in harmony with these conclusions. Bagley, McCall, and Thorndike all make much use of phonetic groupings in their spellers, although the general plans of the books differ greatly. These spellers, together with sixteen others, are analyzed in Chapter IV.

In certain of his studies Gates, while asserting that phonetic generalization is very common, expresses uncertainty as to its value. In the 1922 monograph [4] he found that children spell extensively by phonetic translation and that a child can use phonetic translation and still be a poor speller. Without guidance phonetic generalization certainly does not always function

[1] Suzzallo, Henry and Pearson, Henry Carr, "Comparative Experimental Teaching in Spelling," *Teachers College Record*, XIII (1912), pp. 37-48.

positively. Carroll in his study [3] confirmed this result; he found that both bright and dull children generalize on a phonetic basis and that many errors result from this habit. In addition to this, Gates [5] found that the deaf who, because of their inability to hear, are incapable of making phonetic generalizations, nevertheless attain a high degree of spelling ability in comparison with other linguistic abilities. This fact would indicate that a high degree of spelling ability may be obtained without any phonetic ability. Gates' study [6] of the phonetic elements of his Primary Reading List,[1] showing the unphonetic character of the English language even for primary grades, led him still further to doubt the value of *unguided* phonetic generalization.

In connection with these studies it should be understood that the pupils were given little or no systematic assistance in guiding their generalizations into proper channels and in avoiding misleading precedents.

It is still possible that spelling lists may be so organized on a phonogram basis and instruction be so directed that pupils can make advantageous use of phonetic generalization and avoid many of the most misleading tendencies which cause negative transfer. The purpose of the present study is to ascertain the degree to which phonetic generalization can be used positively and also the extent, in so far as this can be determined by a thorough grade-by-grade analysis of the phonetic and visual elements of the word list.

ANALYSIS OF WORD ELEMENTS ALREADY PUBLISHED

A thorough analysis of a spelling vocabulary, such as has been suggested by Tidyman, Thorndike (see Chapter I) and others, has never been attempted.

Gates [6] summarizes the analyses of word elements with reference to reading. He tells us that Vogel, Jaycoxe, and Washburne counted the frequencies of only two-letter combinations, such as *ee, ed, ea, an, th, sh,* and *gr.* Osburn studied the frequencies of others, such as *co, st, pr,* and *re,* that begin with consonants. These writers also studied the frequency of certain letter combinations possessing certain sounds, but not the fre-

[1] Gates, A. I., *A Reading Vocabulary for the Primary Grades.* Bureau of Publications, Teachers College, Columbia University, New York, 1926.

quency of the same letters having different sounds when combined with other letters. Miss R. E. Atkins made a more comprehensive analysis of a number of two-letter combinations. The study made by Gates [6] was more inclusive than any of these, as he analyzed two-letter, three-letter, and more than three-letter combinations together with the placement in the words of the letter combinations, and also considered whether the letters analyzed came at the beginning, in the middle, or at the end of a word.

The analysis of the spelling list here described is similar to those mentioned. The set-up for this analysis, however, is so arranged that it lends itself to an absolutely thorough analysis of any letter combination, whether of one, two, or more letters, both phonetically and visually. Each grade list can be studied alone or together with other grades. It is also possible by this plan to study any or all words with reference to any rules. The study of rules is described in a later chapter.

Description of an Analysis of a Spelling Vocabulary

Large sheets[1] of squared paper were labeled in columns so that every possible two-letter combination appeared. For example:

the *a* sheet was labeled *aa, ab, ac,* etc., through *az*
the *b* sheet was labeled *ba, bb, bc,* etc., through *bz*
the *c* sheet was labeled *ca, cb, cc,* etc., through *cz*
to
the *z* sheet was labeled *za, zb, zc,* etc., through *zz*

In this way there was one sheet for every letter, or 26 sheets. Each sheet contained 26 columns. The square of 26 is 676, which represents the total number of two-letter combinations that it would be possible to have in the English language. It is interesting to note that this analysis found instances of each of 409 of these possible combinations, leaving 267 columns or two-letter elements not represented in the 4,065 words.

The list of words for the first half of Grade 2 was then entered on the sheets, and each word was written as many times as it had letters minus 1. For example, *HARD* was written under the columns marked *ha, ar,* and *rd,* or three times. When the

[1] See the Appendix for a sample sheet.

words for Grade 2A were all entered on the sheets, a line was drawn across each page under the words in this grade; then Grade 2B was entered in the same way. Grades 2A, 2B, and 3A were placed on one set of sheets, and Grades 3B and 4A on another set of sheets as described above. Beginning with Grade 4B and continuing through 8B a separate set of sheets was allotted each half-grade because some two-letter combinations appeared so frequently that it was impossible to get more than one grade on one set of sheets.

When all the words were entered, the writer with one assistant had transcribed 21,639 words, or a total of 21,639 two-letter visual combinations, excluding the first typed alphabetical list and the tabulations for studying final letters.

This set-up made it possible to examine every two-letter combination in the whole list of words. The single letters could also be studied on their respective sheets. The initial letters, of course, appeared in the first columns. The writer did not, however, include an additional column on every sheet for every final single letter. This was done when needed, for example, for final *s* in the study of plurals. It was also done for such letters as *e* and *y* in the study of rules. This set-up made it unnecessary to write any words again except those that were to be studied for certain phonograms.

When the words were finally recorded, it was possible to make a complete examination of any group of letters of any length, whether of two, three, or more letters, whether suffixes, prefixes, plurals, or any other letter elements. For example, a three-letter combination like *ain* could be found under *ai*; *ught* could be found under *ug*; the prefix *per* under *pe*; or the suffix *tion* under *ti*. By means of this set-up any group of letters could be studied for

1. Grade placement.
2. Frequency within a grade. For example, if a certain rule is found to be useful, such as the *qu* rule, the words could be examined to see in what grade *qu* appeared most frequently; or if the *ie–ei* rule is being analyzed, the frequency and consistency could be studied from the *ie* and the *ei* columns for the grade placement of the words governed by the rule.

The first general question of interest is the frequency of the two-letter elements. The range is from 1 to 499, the digraph *in* appearing 499 times. Table II gives the frequencies by step intervals of twenty. This table shows an extremely skewed distribution. There are 189 two-letter combinations which have a frequency of less than twenty; in other words, over 46 per cent of the 409 two-letter combinations have frequencies of less than twenty in 4,065 words.

It was arbitrarily decided to study more intensively only those two-letter elements that appeared with a frequency of fifty or more. A frequency of fifty means that such a combination appears in fifty out of 4,065 words, or in 1.2 per cent of the words, provided it appears only once in a single word.

TABLE II

FREQUENCY OF APPEARANCE OF ALL TWO-LETTER
ELEMENTS IN THE WORD LIST

Step Interval	Frequency
480–99	1
460–79	0
440–59	0
420–39	2
400–19	0
380–99	0
360–79	0
340–59	2
320–39	1
300–19	1
280–99	2
260–79	5
240–59	3
220–39	2
200–19	3
180–99	4
160–79	10
140–59	7
120–39	10
100–19	22
80–99	14
60–79	31
40–59	36
20–39	64
1–19	189
Total	409

Some two-letter combinations appear two or more times in one word, as *in* in *beginning*. A study of the digraphs with a frequency of fifty or more limited the analysis to 139 of the 409 two-letter combinations found in the word list. Table III gives the 139 digraphs having frequencies of fifty or more. They are arranged in the order of the greatest frequency.

It will be noted that Table III contains 382 different letter combinations as follows:

1. 139 two-letter, with 50 or more frequency.
2. 218 three-letter, with 20 or more frequency,
    plus all three-letter combinations studied by Gates [6], or others mentioned in his book, and
3. 25 four- or more-letter combinations, with a frequency of 20 or more plus those mentioned by Gates [6].

All of these 382 elements were carefully studied for correct pronunciation.

A standard dictionary was constantly referred to until every word was strictly catalogued with reference to its proper pronunciation. If a word had more than one pronunciation it was counted in each case. For example, *read, read, lead, lead,* etc., were entered in both the long *e* and the short *e* columns. These pronunciations were not combined as Gates [6] combined them in reading. The phonogram grouping was made strictly according to a dictionary because:

1. The teacher's pronunciation should as nearly as possible conform to the standard set by a good dictionary. Practically all spellers analyzed in the study of rules (Chapter IV) stressed proper pronunciation.
2. Children should probably learn to use a dictionary. Seventeen of the twenty spellers studied (Chapter IV) emphatically advocated the use of a dictionary.

Table III gives the number of different sounds found for each of these letter combinations. It will be seen that only 20 of the 218 three-letter combinations and only one four-letter element have a frequency of fifty or more. The range in Table III for different pronunciations of the word elements is 1 to 23.

Table IV shows the phonetic analysis of the 139 two-letter elements. Only one two-letter combination has twenty-three

TABLE III

DATA COVERING THE MOST FREQUENT COMBINATIONS AND OTHERS
FREQUENTLY USED IN TEACHING

Word Element	Total Number in 4,065 Words	Total Number of Different Sounds	Word Element	Total Number in 4,065 Words	Total Number of Different Sounds
in	499	7	ta	144	7
re	433	9	si	138	8
er	430	7	ch	137	6
en	347	6	pe	135	9
on	341	12	ca	126	8
te	324	6	ic	126	6
st	302	3	pr	125	1
ed	287	5	as	125	14
ti	285	4	ll	124	2
at	277	23	tio	122	2
ar	275	12	la	121	9
nt	274	5	tion	121	2
le	270	9	us	120	12
es	256	11	lo	117	5
ng	255	4	ly	117	2
an	254	10	di	115	5
se	230	9	ec	115	10
or	221	8	tr	114	1
ea	212	12	et	114	6
ra	208	9	il	112	5
ing	207	2	ge	112	8
co	205	12	ha	111	7
de	198	6	ai	111	4
al	193	13	nc	110	3
io	185	8	sh	106	1
ce	181	6	rt	105	5
ri	178	4	ss	103	3
me	177	6	ac	103	13
ve	176	6	un	103	6
it	173	6	ct	102	4
is	168	9	pa	102	6
ne	167	10	ee	102	2
ro	166	12	om	101	7
el	166	4	ie	101	9
nd	163	1	ho	101	10
li	159	6	po	98	8
th	157	3	ad	92	8
he	156	13	ry	91	2
ion	156	4	bl	91	3
ou	154	9	ni	89	4
ent	150	6	ma	89	8
ur	147	9	em	88	5

TABLE III (*Continued*)

Word Element	Total Number in 4,065 Words	Total Number of Different Sounds	Word Element	Total Number in 4,065 Words	Total Number of Different Sounds
hi	85	5	rr	59	1
to	84	11	ty	59	2
ap	83	7	ut	59	11
ol	83	7	im	58	3
mi	82	3	no	58	9
ow	81	4	wa	58	6
pl	80	2	nce	58	4
ter	79	4	cr	57	3
ir	78	8	rd	57	2
ns	78	3	we	57	9
id	77	5	rea	57	6
be	76	10	ep	56	4
os	76	9	iv	56	3
tu	76	4	pro	56	6
ate	76	10	res	56	6
ig	75	8	ble	56	3
oo	74	5	fa	55	7
fi	73	4	her	55	10
mp	72	1	cu	54	5
mo	71	8	qu	54	2
su	71	11	vi	54	5
ati	71	7	ba	53	7
ci	70	7	op	52	5
gr	70	1	pi	52	3
na	68	5	sc	52	3
pp	68	3	wi	52	3
am	67	6	rn	51	1
gh	67	3	ect	51	3
ot	67	16	com	50	3
ul	67	6	ess	50	2
ck	66	1	sta	50	7
sa	66	7	ine	49	13
con	66	5	ted	49	2
so	65	10	ment	48	2
ab	64	3	ain	47	3
ag	64	9	ver	47	4
ke	64	5	per	46	4
fe	62	6	tin	45	3
fo	62	9	all	44	4
men	62	1	ure	44	7
ex	61	1	ive	43	4
rs	61	3	end	42	2
tt	61	1	ght	42	1
est	61	4	igh	42	3
sp	60	3	the	42	10

TABLE III (*Continued*)

Word Element	Total Number in 4,065 Words	Total Number of Different Sounds	Word Element	Total Number in 4,065 Words	Total Number of Different Sounds
for	41	3	ish	29	1
ear	40	4	tar	29	5
ere	40	8	cha	28	11
int	40	5	ind	28	2
ist	40	6	nti	28	3
nte	40	3	ose	28	6
ran	40	5	tic	28	2
str	40	1	are	27	6
anc	39	5	kin	27	3
and	39	3	lea	27	3
ten	39	2	lin	27	4
ant	38	6	pla	27	3
der	38	1	rin	27	3
abl	37	3	sto	27	8
app	37	1	tte	27	4
ide	37	7	ust	27	2
pre	37	5	act	26	3
tur	37	4	ead	26	2
age	36	7	han	26	2
che	36	10	ple	26	3
eve	36	9	ssi	26	2
nde	36	4	ther	26	2
rat	36	8	att	25	1
tra	36	4	ire	25	2
cti	35	2	lly	25	1
eat	35	9	use	25	7
par	35	4	ass	24	3
ste	35	5	cat	24	7
enc	34	3	din	24	3
dis	33	4	ele	24	7
ight	33	3	ell	24	3
ting	33	1	ies	24	5
art	32	5	ill	24	2
gra	32	2	ite	24	7
rec	32	6	nin	24	2
eas	31	4	rou	24	5
ice	31	8	sen	24	3
pos	31	6	she	24	4
sti	31	2	sin	24	4
und	31	4	ven	24	4
red	30	3	ang	23	4
ard	29	7	arr	23	4
ast	29	7	ath	23	9
eme	29	6	ave	23	8
hin	29	11	car	23	4

TABLE III (*Continued*)

Word Element	Total Number in 4,065 Words	Total Number of Different Sounds	Word Element	Total Number in 4,065 Words	Total Number of Different Sounds
cou	23	6	clo	19	4
den	23	3	ever	19	4
ely	23	1	ick	19	1
ise	23	8	lan	19	4
ner	23	2	nat	19	7
ppe	23	5	pen	19	2
pri	23	4	qui	19	3
sed	23	2	ree	19	1
spe	23	3	shi	19	5
tan	23	2	ake	18	2
thi	23	5	cal	18	4
ugh	23	7	king	18	1
ach	22	7	led	18	4
ail	22	1	mis	18	3
ery	22	2	nal	18	2
exp	22	1	nes	18	3
low	22	3	por	18	4
sho	22	7	rel	18	3
tai	22	3	ren	18	4
tat	22	3	rep	18	2
tch	22	1	ret	18	5
tri	22	2	ser	18	4
ture	22	2	iou	17	2
min	22	3	mar	17	5
ned	22	2	pin	17	3
ame	21	7	rri	17	2
cor	21	4	air	16	2
ful	21	1	duc	16	3
ins	21	4	eae	16	3
lar	21	4	even	16	4
man	21	3	gre	16	4
mer	21	4	hing	16	5
mpl	21	2	nst	16	1
sio	21	2	ring	16	1
sion	21	2	son	16	4
ack	20	1	tain	16	2
can	20	3	tal	16	4
hea	20	7	ual	16	3
pea	20	3	win	16	5
rem	20	4	wor	16	3
row	20	2	atu	15	7
sit	20	4	let	15	3
sur	20	4	bli	14	2
tre	20	3	tho	14	7
ase	19	6	ded	13	2

TABLE III (*Continued*)

Word Element	Total Number in 4,065 Words	Total Number of Different Sounds	Word Element	Total Number in 4,065 Words	Total Number of Different Sounds
nit	13	4	ark	8	1
oose	13	2	ink	8	2
over	13	2	rain	8	1
ster	13	2	fur	7	1
atc	12	2	has	7	3
hat	12	2	ior	7	3
ref	12	3	fun	6	2
tiv	12	1	ould	6	2
eep	11	1	good	5	1
err	11	3	ought	5	1
gro	11	3	oak	2	1
tive	11	1	then	2	1
rest	10	1	leaf	1	1
hand	9	4			

different pronunciations in this word list. Table III shows that this digraph is *at*, with a frequency of 277. Another digraph, shown by Table IV as having sixteen different pronunciations, is found, by referring to Table III, to be *ot*. By using Tables III and IV the reader can study each individual digraph for frequency and number of pronunciations. Eleven of the 139 digraphs have only one pronunciation. These digraphs are *ck, ex, gr, mp, nd, pr, rn, rr, sh, tr,* and *tt*. It is significant that only one of these digraphs contains a vowel.

An interesting conclusion drawn from Table IV is that the 139 digraphs have a total of 870 pronunciations or each digraph has an average of six different pronunciations. (See Appendix for a typical phonogram sheet.)

In the description of an analysis of a Spelling Vocabulary it was shown that the original sheets give the frequencies by grades for all the word elements. Table V is included in this study to show the frequency by grades of the first 22 word elements listed in Table III. It would be impossible in this brief study to include all such data. It is possible from the original sheets to locate both the grade in which there is the greatest frequency for any word element and the grade in which any word element has the greatest number of different sounds.

TABLE IV

DIGRAPHS HAVING A FREQUENCY OF 50 OR MORE AND THE NUMBER OF
DIFFERENT WAYS THEY ARE PRONOUNCED ACCORDING TO A
STANDARD DICTIONARY (WEBSTER)

Number of Different Sounds	Frequency	Sound × Frequency
23	1	23
22	0	0
21	0	0
20	0	0
19	0	0
18	0	0
17	0	0
16	1	16
15	0	0
14	1	14
13	3	39
12	6	72
11	4	44
10	6	60
9	15	135
8	11	88
7	11	77
6	17	102
5	15	75
4	11	44
3	18	54
2	8	16
1	11	11
Total	139	870

The writer has not exhausted the possibility for study of the word elements, but has arbitrarily set limits which are conservative. All word elements affecting at least 1 per cent of all the words were studied, plus any other word elements longer than the digraphs that had appeared in analyses for reading but were not so frequent as to be found in 1 per cent of the words in this list.

The suggestion given by Thorndike [13] and quoted in Chapter I, prompted the writer to make a study of all the vowel combinations in the two-letter elements.

The greatest number of times a letter can be combined with any other single letter is two times twenty-six minus one, or fifty-one. The frequency of appearance of the five vowels is as follows:

a .... 46 out of the possible 51
e .... 49 out of the possible 51
i .... 45 out of the possible 51
o .... 47 out of the possible 51
u .... 42 out of the possible 51

TABLE V

FREQUENCIES BY GRADE OF THE TWENTY-TWO LETTER COMBINATIONS
HAVING THE HIGHEST TOTAL FREQUENCIES IN THE VISUAL ANALYSIS

Word Element	2A	2B	3A	3B	4A	4B	5A	5B	6A	6B	7A	7B	8A	8B	Total
in	9	16	39	32	33	31	41	48	49	30	40	36	56	39	499
re	8	10	9	9	19	22	29	37	37	44	60	53	39	57	433
er	12	15	6	8	23	19	46	48	37	46	46	48	35	41	430
en	5	10	8	5	12	20	23	29	25	39	48	42	32	49	347
on	4	3	11	10	12	14	22	15	16	23	40	54	64	53	341
te	5	9	11	8	16	17	22	24	22	31	31	47	39	42	324
st	6	15	14	14	24	19	30	14	25	22	26	29	35	29	302
ed	2	8	16	27	16	12	10	22	25	24	31	31	36	27	287
ti	0	4	7	7	9	5	14	14	16	19	31	47	55	57	285
at	11	5	5	8	20	13	10	16	14	22	30	38	41	44	277
ar	10	6	12	13	14	20	27	16	24	29	32	22	23	27	275
nt	2	6	8	10	9	12	17	19	23	27	36	40	30	35	274
le	5	6	10	16	23	19	22	27	25	23	28	26	19	21	270
es	3	7	11	6	14	24	18	20	19	22	23	32	20	37	256
ng	4	11	28	23	21	24	25	30	31	13	11	4	22	8	255
an	6	10	8	11	15	19	22	23	22	19	16	28	25	30	254
se	2	4	12	11	13	16	18	26	11	26	28	24	25	14	230
or	3	7	9	10	12	7	13	12	18	26	21	25	26	32	221
ea	5	6	17	16	23	16	19	27	19	12	17	15	10	10	212
ra	2	5	4	8	14	17	18	14	19	19	17	25	19	27	208
ing	4	9	22	22	15	20	23	23	22	9	9	4	19	6	207
co	2	6	5	3	10	5	5	9	17	22	24	19	34	44	205

The digraphs containing vowels which never appeared in this word list are:

a .... aa ae aj qa aq
e .... ae qe
i .... ih ii ij qi iw iy
o .... oj oq qo xo
u .... uh uj ku uu uv uw wu yu zu

The following tabulation shows the number of times that each of the vowel digraphs appears with a frequency of fifty or more. Their exact frequencies are shown in Table III.

a 25

e . . . . 29 minus *ea* because counted under *a*, above

i . . . . 26 minus *ai* and *ie*

o . . . . 21 minus *io*

u . . . . 10 minus *ou*

Total   111

The total, 111, minus 5 that were counted twice, equals 106; therefore, 33 consonant digraphs rank among those of frequency of fifty or more. Table III gives the frequency of each of the above vowel digraphs and the number of pronunciations for each. In Table V only three consonant digraphs, *st*, *nt*, and *ng*, appear, and the number of different pronunciations are 3, 5, and 4, respectively.

Summary

The analysis of phonetic elements (Table III) has shown the frequency of such combinations as *in*, *re*, *er*, *en*, *on*, *te*, *st*, *ed*, *ti*, *at*, etc. It also has shown the number of ways that such elements can be pronounced. Of the twenty-two word elements having a frequency of over two hundred, only one has as few as two pronunciations. The most frequent digraph, *in*, can be pronounced in seven ways. The digraph *at* is pronounced in twenty-three ways.

Do these data help to explain why the child may not always spell words that he really knows when they are merely pronounced for him by another person?

Table III shows in general that three-letter or longer word elements are less frequent in appearance and have relatively fewer sounds than the two-letter elements. The analysis of vowel digraphs shows that the vowel *e* appears more frequently than any other vowel. It appears in nine of the twenty-two word elements tabulated in Table V.

Finally, the practical determination of the usefulness of phonetic and visual generalization is still unsolved. The data here given, however, comprise essential material for use in an experimental study.

CHAPTER IV

GENERALIZATION BASED ON SPELLING RULES

SELECTION OF THE RULES

In order to determine what spelling rules are being commonly taught, twenty spellers (listed at the end of this chapter) were selected and thoroughly studied. When this investigation was begun these twenty spellers represented all those catalogued in the Teachers College Library at Columbia University which had been published since 1920. These books were also chosen to include texts for the teaching of spelling from the first grade through the high school. Two of the spellers, the one by Arnold and the one by Trowbridge, were marked "High School Spellers." There was nothing to indicate whether or not these spellers were meant for both junior and senior high schools. Since the word list in this study was designed for Grades 2 through 8, it was necessary to check these two spellers to see if the same words appeared in them. They were found to have largely the same words except that both stressed all derived forms while the 4,065 words under investigation did not contain all the derivatives.

The twenty spellers were carefully analyzed to determine, first, the source of words taught; second, the suggested methods of teaching; third, the use of the dictionary; fourth, the use of drill in tests; and fifth, the number of rules and definitions listed and the author's method of presentation of rules and definitions. The last-named step is the one most pertinent to this study. The purpose of this chapter, therefore, is to record the findings of the analysis of these rules.

In the tables used in this chapter the name of the author will represent the book under discussion. In the case of co-authors, the first name in the series will be used. Table VI lists the spellers, indicates the grades, and gives the number of rules and definitions used by each speller. It is interesting to note from this table the following facts:

27

2 spellers had no rules or definitions
7 spellers had 1 to 19 rules or definitions
3 spellers had 20 to 29 rules or definitions
4 spellers had 30 to 39 rules or definitions
4 spellers had 40 to 48 rules or definitions

TABLE VI

DESCRIPTION OF SPELLERS

Author	Grade	Number of Rules and Definitions
1. Alexander	Grades 7 and 8 and Advanced	16
2. Arnold	High School	30
3. Board of education, New York City	Grades 2–8	19
4. Breed	Complete course, Grades 1–8	3
5. Brown	Junior High School, Grades 7, 8, 9	0
6. Horn	Grades 1–8	0
7. Jones	Complete course, Grades 1–8	1
8. Kallom	Grades 1–7	27
9. Leonard	Advanced Grades 7–8	24
10. Lewis	Grades 1–8	43
11. McCall	Grades 1–8	48
12. Phillips	Grades 1–8	2
13. Ramsay	Grades 1–8	11
14. Reeder	Junior High School (grades not stated)	40
15. Smith	Grades 7–9	33
16. Starch	Grades 2–8	28
17. Thorndike	Grades 2–8	48
18. Tidyman	Grades 1–7	13
19. Trabue	Grades 2–9	39
20. Trowbridge	High School	30
Author unknown*		2
Total		457

* It will be observed that two rules in this table are listed "author unknown." This is due to an error made in writing the name of the author after the rule. The method of tabulating makes it certain that neither of these two rules could have appeared in more than one speller. It seemed unnecessary to check this error because the frequency of the rule would not be high enough to be pertinent to this study.

Table VII gives the frequency of use of the rules and definitions in the spellers. Inspection of this table reveals a number of interesting facts. The range of frequency is from 1 to 15. One hundred ten separate rules and definitions were used by the

TABLE VII

Frequency of Use	Number of Rules	Rules Multiplied by Frequency
?	2	2
1	33	33
2	15	30
3	12	36
4	10	40
5	11	55
6	4	24
7	2	14
8	4	32
9	5	45
10	2	20
11	2	22
12	5	60
13	0	0
14	1	14
15	2	30
Total	110	457

twenty spellers, but seventy-two of them appeared in four or less than four spellers. The total of 457 rules and definitions indicates that, on the average, a rule is used four times. Thirty-three rules and definitions were used only once.[1] Two rules, however, appear to be important enough for fifteen different authors to include them in their spellers.

The 110 different rules and definitions were tabulated according to the types of rules and definitions. Table VIII gives the number appearing under each heading. For example, in the twenty spellers there were 6 general statements about words of one syllable, 17 statements about words of more than one syllable, 15 statements about capital letters, and 24 statements about suffixes. According to this table, the 110 generalized statements are classified under nineteen separate categories.

It was arbitrarily decided that no rule or definition would be carefully studied which was not used by at least five of the spellers. Thirty-eight rules and definitions were found to be used by five or more of the spellers and accordingly were ana-

[1] There were really thirty-five rules and definitions that were used only once, since again two rules appear with "no author."

30 *Generalization in Spelling*

TABLE VIII

RULES AND DEFINITIONS USED IN THE SPELLERS

Type	Total Number in Spellers	Number in Five or More Spellers	Statement in Five or More Spellers Classified as	
			Rule	Definition
1. Abbreviations	4	2	1	1
2. Accent	1	1	0	0
3. Alphabet	1	0	0	0
4. Antonyms	1	1	0	1
5. Apostrophe	2	2	2	0
6. Capital letters (use of)	15	3	3	0
7. Compound words	3	1	0	1
8. Derivatives	2	1	0	1
9. Homonyms	1	1	0	1
10. Hyphen	3	2	2	0
11. Letters	11	3	3	0
12. Plurals	12	4	3	1
13. Prefixes	4	1	0	1
14. Rhymes	1	0	0	0
15. Root	1	1	0	1
16. Suffixes	24	11	10	1
17. Syllables, more than one	17	2	2	0
18. Syllables, one	6	1	1	0
19. Synonyms	1	1	0	1
Total	110	38	27	10

lyzed. These are recorded below. The figure following each statement indicates the number of spellers using it.

I. The plural of most nouns is formed by adding *s* or *es* to the singular. [15]

II. Final *e* is dropped before a suffix beginning with a vowel. (*hoping*) [15]

III. Sometimes when we write two words together we leave out one or more letters. The apostrophe is used to show where a letter or letters have been omitted. Such words are called contractions. [14]

IV. Nouns ending in final *y* preceded by a consonant change *y* to *i* and add *es* to form the plural. [12]

V. A syllable or combination of syllables added at the beginning of a word is called a prefix. [12]

VI. Abbreviations are always followed by a period. [12]

VII. To show that a syllable is pronounced with more force, it is followed by this mark ('), called an accent. [12]

VIII. Monosyllables or words accented on the last syllable ending in a single consonant preceded by a single vowel, or a vowel after *qu*, double the final consonant when adding a suffix beginning with a vowel. If this accent is not on the last syllable, the final consonant is usually not doubled. [12]

IX. *I* before *e* except after *c* or when sounded as *a*, as in *neighbor* and *weigh*. [11]

X. A syllable or syllables added to the end of a word is called a suffix. [11]

XI. Proper nouns and adjectives formed from proper nouns should always begin with capital letters. [10]

XII. The apostrophe is used to show possession, as *father's*. [10]

XIII. A compound word is a word made up of two or more distinct words, used as one word in form and meaning. (*railroad*) [9]

XIV. In words like *calf* and *half* the *f* of the singular is changed to *v* before adding *es* to form the plural. [9]

XV. Final *e* is kept before a suffix beginning with a consonant. (*careful*) [9]

XVI. When words end in a single consonant preceded by a single vowel, the last consonant is called a final consonant. This final consonant is doubled before a suffix beginning with a vowel. [9]

XVII. When final *y* is preceded by a consonant the *y* is changed to *i* when adding a suffix beginning with a consonant. [9]

XVIII. When two words mean the same thing, we say they are synonyms. [8]

XIX. Homonyms are words which are pronounced the same, but which differ in spelling and meaning. [8]

XX. The hyphen is always used in writing the words for numbers like *twenty-five*. [8]

XXI. Final *y* is changed to *i* before any suffix that does not begin with *i*. In *carriage, marriage,* and like words final *y* is changed to *i* before a suffix beginning with a vowel. [8]

XXII. A word used as a base to which a prefix or a suffix is added is called a root. [7]

XXIII. Words ending with the suffix *ful* have only one *l* at the end. [7]

XXIV. Letter *q* is always followed by letter *u*. [6]

XXV. The names of the months of the year always begin with capital letters. [6]

XXVI. A derivative is a word that has been built up from another word by the addition of a suffix or a prefix or both. [6]

XXVII. In letters and in other writing we often shorten a word. This is called the abbreviation of the word. [6]

XXVIII. Words of one syllable having the long sound of the vowel usually end in silent *e*. [5]

XXIX. Every syllable must contain a sounded vowel. [5]

XXX. When dividing words into syllables, prefixes and suffixes are separated from their roots when the prefix or suffix contains a sounded vowel. [5]

XXXI. *Ph* often sounds like *f*. [5]

XXXII. The names of the days of the week always begin with capital letters. [5]

XXXIII. A word that means more than one is called a plural word. [5]

XXXIV. When two words mean opposite things we call them antonyms. [5]

XXXV. A hyphen is used at the end of the line to indicate that a portion of the word is found at the beginning of the next line. [5]

XXXVI. The final *e* is dropped before the suffix *er*; otherwise there would be two *e*'s. [5]

XXXVII. A word ending in *y* after a vowel usually retains the *y* before any suffix. [5]

XXXVIII. In adding *ing* to a word ending in *ie*, drop the final *e* and change *i* to *y*, as *tie*, *tying*. [5]

Keeping in mind the definitions of the words *rule* and *definition*, each generalized statement was carefully scrutinized to see whether it was actually a rule or a definition. Since this study is concerned with the use of rules in spellers, it was decided to eliminate all the generalized statements which did not fit the definition given for a *rule*. According to a standard dictionary the term *definition* means the description of a thing by its properties; as used here, it denotes the act of making clear or the explanation of a meaning of a word or term. The word *rule* means the guide for action; in this study it is used to express a general principle concerning the formation or use of words by a concise statement thereof, for example, a rule for forming the plurals of nouns.

On the basis of these two definitions, eleven of the thirty-eight generalized statements were eliminated. There remained twenty-seven rules to be analyzed with reference to the 4,065 words under consideration. The last two columns of Table VIII give the number of rules and definitions appearing in five or more spellers. It is an interesting and perhaps significant fact that rules concerning suffixes seem to be decidedly the ones most frequently used in modern spellers. The third column of Table VIII shows that ten of the twenty-seven rules deal with suffixes. Three rules each concerning letters, capital letters, and plurals gain second place in popularity with textbook writers. Two rules each on words of more than one syllable, the hyphen, and the apostrophe are used in five or more spellers while one rule for the use of abbreviations and one on words of one syllable are among those included in this study.

Analysis of the Rules Selected

A detailed analysis of the generalized statements which come strictly under the term *rule* was undertaken. It was mentioned above that this study was concerned with rules only. A second reason for the elimination of definitions was that they do not give the children directions for spelling words. A definition makes an explanation, only; for example, eleven spellers had "a syllable or syllables added at the end of the word is called a suffix." Fifteen spellers had "final *e* is dropped before a suffix beginning with a vowel." The latter statement was thought of as a rule, while the former was considered a definition. Although both are generalized statements, this study is limited to an analysis of the rule in the strictest sense.

No derivatives and no compound words that are not already listed in the 4,065 words were included in this analysis because their spelling difficulty had not been determined and hence they could not be assigned grade placements. In general, it will be seen that those derivatives that do appear in this list of words are from one to three grades displaced from their root words and are, on the whole, placed in higher rather than lower grades. The rules and the discussion of their analyses are presented in the order of the greatest frequency of use of the rules in the spellers. The figures appearing after each rule represent the number of spellers in which the rule was found.

Rule I.—The plural of most nouns is formed by adding *s* or *es* to the singular. [15]

There are 125 words in the 4,065 studied which have plurals formed by adding *s* or *es* to the singular. The grade placement of the singulars and their plurals appears by grades in Table IX. The deviation of the plural from the grade placement of the singular is as follows: 34 plurals are at the same grade placement as the singulars, 65 deviate one grade from the singulars, 20 deviate two grades, 3 deviate three grades, and 3 deviate four grades. Only 10 of these plurals are at a lower grade placement then their singulars. The grade of greatest frequency for the singulars is the second, while the grade of greatest frequency of plurals is the fourth. Fifty per cent of the plurals fall below Grade 5. There are twenty-five singulars which have plurals that are not formed according to Rule I. Eight of the exceptions are: *gentlemen, men, mice, geese, teeth, women, leaves,* and *lives.* Sixteen of the exceptions come under Rule IV and one plural, although it is not a noun plural, comes under Rule XIV.

TABLE IX
GRADE PLACEMENT OF WORDS GOVERNED BY RULE I

Grade	Singulars	Plurals
Grade 2	24	3
Grade 3	22	18
Grade 4	23	37
Grade 5	19	17
Grade 6	19	12
Grade 7	16	18
Grade 8	2	20
Total	125	125

Rule II.[1]—Final *e* is dropped before a suffix beginning with a vowel. [15]

In connection with this rule all root words were counted that had one or more derivatives resulting from the adding of the following suffixes, *able, al, ar, ate, ed, ery, est, ial, ible, ice, inal, ing, ion, ior, ish, ity, ive, or, ous, ow, ure,* and *y.* There are actually 804 words that have final *e.* Only 137 of these words have derived forms governed by this rule. There are 167 such derivatives and four exceptions to the rule. Table X gives the summary for Rule II by grades.

Rule III.—Sometimes when we write two words together we leave out one or more letters. The apostrophe is used to show where a letter or letters have been omitted. Such words are called contractions. [14]

The total number of words governed by this rule is 20. Their grade placement is shown in Table XI. There are no exceptions.

Rule IV.—Nouns ending in final *y* preceded by a consonant change *y* to *i* and add *es* to form the plural. [12]

There are 308 words ending in *y* preceded by a consonant. A

[1] Notice that Rule II governs suffixes beginning with a vowel while Rule XV governs those beginning with a consonant. In making the analysis for these two rules the following words were not included: compound words that change in meaning as *dine—dinner,* and all words having only a visual configuration such as *grave—gravy, police—policy* and *pie—piece.* Plurals were not counted because it was assumed that only *s* was added, and not *es.* (See Rule I.)

TABLE X

SUMMARY FOR RULE II

Grade	Roots	Derivatives	Exceptions
Grade 2	8	2	0
Grade 3	22	14	0
Grade 4	15	11	2
Grade 5	19	26	1
Grade 6	31	23	0
Grade 7	31	42	1
Grade 8	11	49	0
Total	137	167	4

TABLE XI

GRADE PLACEMENT OF WORDS GOVERNED
BY RULE III

Grade	Frequency
Grade 2	1
Grade 3	5
Grade 4	5
Grade 5	5
Grade 6	2
Grade 7	2
Total	20

few of these words are nouns whose plurals would come under this rule if they were in the word list. Many of the words are adjectives, as *dirty, dusty, sleepy*; many others are adverbs ending in *ly* and a few are verbs, as *marry*. The sixteen nouns with plurals in *ies* which are in the list are placed in the grades as shown in Table XII. There are no exceptions to this rule. Notice in Table XII that the plurals appear from half a grade to three grades beyond the singulars. There are two exceptions at the sixth grade—*factory* and *enemy*; their plurals appear in the same grade. There are three more words ending in *ies* in the word list, two of which are strictly verbs—*carries* and *applies*, and their plurals are among the 4,065 words. The third word is *facilities*, there being no singular in the word list.

To summarize, there are 19 words, not all of which are nouns, that could be governed by this rule if the rule were changed to read, "*Words* ending in final *y*, preceded by a consonant, change *y* to *i* when adding the suffix *es*," instead of, "*Nouns* ending in final *y*," etc. There are 130 words, nouns and verbs, in the 308 besides those that have already been analyzed that could have derivatives formed by changing *y* to *i* and adding *es*, but such derivatives do not appear in the list. There are only sixteen

TABLE XII

SUMMARY FOR RULE IV

Grade	Singulars	Plurals
Grade 2	2	0
Grade 3	3	1
Grade 4	3	2
Grade 5	2	4
Grade 6	3	4
Grade 7	2	0
Grade 8	1	5
Total	16	16

opportunities to use this rule; these are scattered over five grades with only two derivatives at the same grade level as the root words. It is rather doubtful whether this rule would be of much value to children unless they could get more practice in using it than they would get from a speller containing only this list of words.

Rule VI.—Abbreviations are always followed by a period. [12]

There are fourteen .abbreviations whose appearances in the grades are shown in Table XIII. There are no exceptions to this rule.

Rule VIII.—Monosyllables or words accented on the last syllable ending in a single consonant preceded by a single vowel, or a vowel after *qu*, double the final consonant when adding a suffix beginning with a vowel. If the accent is not on the last syllable, the final consonant usually is not doubled. [12]

Two words with *qu* in the list come under this rule. There are 752 double letters in the 4,065 words being studied. There are fifty-two root words having fifty-eight derivatives governed by this rule. Some of the root words have more than one derived form. Out of the fifty-eight derivatives governed by this rule, thirteen are not accented on the last syllable but double the final letter when adding a suffix beginning with a vowel. If it were not for the word *usually*, which appears in the last sentence of the rule, these thirteen derived forms would be considered exceptions. Fourteen words having double letters would enter

TABLE XIII

SUMMARY FOR RULE VI

Grade	Frequency
Grade 4	4
Grade 5	1
Grade 6	3
Grade 7	1
Grade 8	5
Total	14

into this count but the root words do not appear in the list. Twenty-two other words in the list have thirty-three derived forms. They are monosyllables or are accented on the last syllable, yet they do not double the final consonant when adding a suffix beginning with a vowel. They end in *w, x,* or *y.* Must the children studying this list of words assume that these three letters are vowels? If not, these twenty-two words are surely exceptions to Rule VIII. The word *travel* is spelled in modern dictionaries with either one or two *l*'s in adding a suffix beginning with a vowel. In this list of words its derivatives, *traveler* and *traveling*, are spelled with one *l* and are placed in the sixth grade. Also, at least ten words in the list are monosyllables or are accented on the last syllable, but they do not have derivatives.

Summarizing this rule we must think of it as follows: To fit the rule

1. Words must be monosyllables or be accented on the last syllable "usually."
2. Words must end in a single consonant.
3. The consonant must be preceded by a single vowel, there being one exception, *qu.*

The rule seems more confusing than helpful. It may be harder to learn the rule and its exceptions than to learn to spell the words separately. There are 752 double letters in the 4,065 words and only 58 plus 14 words, or a total of 73 words, that can be considered as conforming to this rule; while 13 of these 73 words plus 22 others in the list are exceptions on the basis of one or more of the criteria just stated.

Table XIV gives a summary of the fifty-two root and fifty-eight derived forms and shows the grade placement of the thirteen words not accented on the last syllable. The other twenty-two words whose thirty-three derived forms are really exceptions do not appear in this table. The differences in grade placement between the roots and the derivatives governed by Rule VIII are as follows: only 8 of the derivatives are in the same grade as the roots; 24 are one grade removed from the root, and only one of these words is below its root. The other derivatives are from two to five grades beyond the root words. These derived forms are, therefore, with the exception of nine words, much more difficult than their roots.

Rule IX.—I before *e* except after *c* or when sounded as *a*, as in *neighbor* and *weigh.* [11]

In order to study this rule, it was necessary to count both *ie* and *ei.* Therefore, the total number of words governed by this rule is 131, 101 words containing *ie* and 30 containing *ei.* Table XV gives the grade placement of both *ie* and *ei.* Thirteen

TABLE XIV

GRADE PLACEMENT OF WORDS REGULARLY GOVERNED BY RULE VIII

Grade	Roots	Derivatives	Exceptions*
Grade 2	13	1	..
Grade 3	11	5	..
Grade 4	5	8	..
Grade 5	5	8	1
Grade 6	6	12	3
Grade 7 ....:	11	3	3
Grade 8	1	8	6
Total	52	45	13

* By exceptions is meant those words which usually would not double the final consonant according to the latter part of the rule.

of the words having *ei* have the sound of *a* and eight of the *ei* conform to the *e* after *c*; therefore, there are nine exceptions to the rule from the standpoint of *ei*. The exceptions are *being, seeing, either, neither, foreign, height, seize, foreigner,* and

TABLE XV

SUMMARY FOR RULE IX

Grade	Frequency of *ie*	Frequency of *ei*
Grade 2	0	1
Grade 3	12	0
Grade 4	7	4
Grade 5	20	8
Grade 6	22	8
Grade 7	16	4
Grade 8	24	5
Total	101	30

leisure. Furthermore, there are eight exceptions in the *ie* words where *i* follows *c* as: *society, science, vacancies, ancient, conscience, efficiency, sufficient,* and *conscientious.* These exceptions appear with reference to grades as follows:

Grade	Frequency of Exceptions
Grade 4	2
Grade 5	2
Grade 6	2
Grade 7	3
Grade 8	8
Total	17

Counting the thirteen words that sound like *a* and thinking only in terms of visual appearance, there are thirty words out of 131 that do not conform to the rule.

Rule XI.—Proper nouns and adjectives formed from proper nouns, should always begin with capital letters. [10]

There are twenty-one words under this rule and no exceptions. The range of placement is from Grade 2 through Grade 8, the greatest frequency being at Grades 5 and 6. Five words appear at each of these grade levels. Table XVI gives the grade location for these words. There are thirty-one other words begin-

TABLE XVI

GRADE PLACEMENT OF RULE XI

Grade	Frequency
Grade 2	1
Grade 3	1
Grade 4	1
Grade 5	5
Grade 6	5
Grade 7	4
Grade 8	4
Total	21

ning with capitals which are governed by Rules XXV and XXXII and are discussed later. Twelve other words or abbreviations in the list have capitals but are not governed by the rules being analyzed. They are *Miss, Mr., Mrs., Ave., P.S., Co., C.O.D., Dept., Dr., Inst., Jan.,* and *Xmas.*

Rule XII.—The apostrophe is used to show possession, as *father's.* [10]

Two words come under this rule, one at Grade 3 and one at Grade 5. There are no exceptions unless one would consider certain possessive words exceptions, such as the pronouns *my, mine, hers, his,* etc.

Rule XIV.—In words like *calf* and *half* the *f* of the singular is changed to *v* before adding *es* to form the plural. [9]

Among the 4,065 words there are eleven that end in *lf.* Only one has a plural in the list. It is *yourself* in the fifth grade list and *yourselves* is in the sixth grade list. The other ten words and their grade placement are as follows:

half 3A	*himself* 4A	*herself* 5A
calf 3B	*myself* 4A	*wolf* 5A
	shelf 4B	*itself* 5B
		self 5B

Rule XV.—Final *e* is kept before a suffix beginning with a consonant, as *careful.* [9]

All root words and their derivatives were counted. The following groups of letters beginning with a consonant were considered as suffixes: *ful, l, less, ly, ment, n, nd, nt, s, son, sque,*

TABLE XVII

SUMMARY FOR RULE XV

Grade	Roots	Derivatives	Exceptions
Grade 2	18	2	2
Grade 3	18	9	0
Grade 4	15	18	2
Grade 5	12	17	2
Grade 6	26	17	6
Grade 7	20	22	7
Grade 8	5	13	9
Total	114	98	28

t, teen, ten, th, tion, tril, and *ty.* The suffix *es* was considered as *s*, since this rule deals with words ending in a final *e*. Table XVII shows the roots, derivatives, and exceptions.

Rule XVI.—When words end in a single consonant preceded by a single vowel, the last consonant is called a final consonant. This final consonant is doubled before a suffix beginning with a vowel. [9]

Rule XVI is only another statement of Rule VIII. Rule VIII includes the letter combination *qu* and a qualifying statement about accents. It will be noted that Rule VIII is used in twelve spellers and Rule XVI is used in nine. Six of the spellers using Rule XVI also use Rule VIII. There were only two words having the two-letter combination *qu* in the list. Subtraction of

TABLE XVIII

SUMMARY FOR RULE XVII

Grade	Roots	Derivatives
Grade 2	0	..
Grade 3	2	..
Grade 4	1	..
Grade 5	1	1
Grade 6	1	1
Grade 7	0	2
Grade 8	2	3
Total	7	7

these two words from the words governed by Rule VIII gives the data for Rule XVI.

Rule XVII.—When final *y* is preceded by a consonant the *y* is changed to *i* when adding a suffix beginning with a consonant. [9]

When the words covered by Rule IV are subtracted from the 308 words ending in *y* preceded by a consonant there are left 292 words. The suffixes beginning with a consonant are *ly, ness, ful, ty,* and *ze.* Seven derived forms and seven roots come under this rule.

There are no exceptions. The grade placement of the root words ranges from the third through the eighth grades, while the derived forms are found in Grades 5 to 8. The derived forms tend to be placed at grades higher than their roots. Table XVIII gives the exact placement.

Rule XX.—The hyphen is always used in writing the words for numbers like twenty-five. [8]

Only two hyphenated words appear in the list, *good-bye* (not a number) at Grade 4.9 and *twenty-five* at Grade 4.8. There are no exceptions to this rule because no other such numbers are given. The only numbers given are *twenty, thirty, forty,* etc.

Rule XXI.—Final *y* is changed to *i* before any suffix that does not begin with *i.* In *carriage,* and *marriage,* and like words, final *y* is changed to *i* before a suffix beginning with a vowel. [8]

This rule is contradictory to Rules IV and XVII as it is here stated, because it does not specify "preceded by consonant." It further contradicts Rule XVII by not stating "suffixes be-

TABLE XIX

SUMMARY FOR RULE XXI

Grade	Roots	Derivatives	Exceptions
Grade 2	0	0	..
Grade 3	5	1	..
Grade 4	0	1	..
Grade 5	2	4	..
Grade 6	6	6	..
Grade 7	2	3	1
Grade 8	1	1	..
Total	16	16	1

ginning with a consonant." Apparently this rule is an attempt to cover exceptions, such as *marriage* and *carriage*, or to cover certain suffixes beginning with vowels, as *age*. Assuming that this rule refers to words ending in final *y* preceded by a consonant and suffixes beginning with vowels, Table XIX shows the number of root words and derivatives, and their grade placement. The suffixes counted are *ed, est, er, age, al, ous,* and *able*. The suffix *es* is not included as it is cared for under Rule IV.

Rule XXIII.—All words ending with suffix *ful* have only one *l* at the end. [7]

A total of sixteen words come under this rule. Their grade placement is shown in Table XX. There are no exceptions.

Rule XXIV.—Letter *q* is always followed by letter *u*. [6]

This rule has no exceptions in the list. As far as the writer has been able to determine, it has no exceptions in the English language. There are fifty-four words under this rule. Their grade placement is shown in Table XXI.

Rule XXV.—The names of the months of the year always begin with capital letters. [6]

This rule has no exceptions. Only twelve words can be governed by this rule. Table XXII gives their grade placement.

Rule XXVIII.—Words of one syllable having the long sound of the vowel usually end in silent *e*. [5]

There are 248 words which consistently follow this rule. There are seventy-nine words which end in final *e* but do not have the long sound of the vowel. Also 260 one-syllable words do not end in *e* and yet have the long sound of the vowel. Examples of these last words are *reach, reel, read, reed, rain, grain, road,*

TABLE XX

SUMMARY FOR RULE XXIII

Grade	Frequency
Grade 4	2
Grade 5	6
Grade 6	4
Grade 7	3
Grade 8	1
Total	16

TABLE XXI
SUMMARY FOR RULE XXIV

Grade	Frequency
Grade 4	8
Grade 5	6
Grade 6	7
Grade 7	12
Grade 8	21
Total	54

TABLE XXII
SUMMARY FOR RULE XXV

Grade	Frequency
Grade 4	2
Grade 5	10
Total	12

sail, bow, say, seat, sight, sleep, spear, and *stain.* It must be confusing to the child to try to distinguish which of the vowels carries the long sound in the words that do end in silent *e* and seem to fit the rule, such as *seize, siege, cease,* and *league.* For instance, the first two words might just as consistently have the long *i* sound, while the last two words might just as consistently have the long *a* sound. Table XXIII gives the grade placement of these words.

Rule XXIX.—Every syllable must contain a sounded vowel. [5]

This rule was not analyzed.

Rule XXX.—When dividing words into syllables, prefixes and suffixes are separated from their roots when the prefix or the suffix contains a sounded vowel. [5]

These last two statements seem to lie on the border line between a rule and a definition as interpreted in this study, and therefore they do not lend themselves to the type of analysis here undertaken. If they are rules, they apply to pronunciation rather than to learning how to spell.

TABLE XXIII

SUMMARY FOR RULE XXVIII

Grade	Roots	Exceptions Ending in *e*	Exceptions with Long Sound Not Ending in *e*
Grade 2	42	16	43
Grade 3	50	13	68
Grade 4	59	13	64
Grade 5	50	18	48
Grade 6	32	11	26
Grade 7	13	7	7
Grade 8	2	1	4
Total	248	79	260

Rule XXXI.—Ph often sounds like *f*. [5]

There are twenty-two words containing the digraph *ph*. Twenty of these sound like *f*. Two of them are separated by syllabication and do not take the sound of *f*, *shepherd*, and *upheld*. Table XXIV gives the grade placement of these words. The two exceptions are at Grade 8.

Rule XXXII.—The names of the days of the week always begin with capital letters. [5]

This rule is, of course, limited to seven words. Table XXV gives the grade placement.

Rule XXXV.—A hyphen is used at the end of the line to indicate that a portion of the word is found at the beginning of the next line. [5]

This rule applies in spelling only when there are dictation exercises.

Rule XXXVI.—The final *e* is dropped before the suffix *er*; otherwise, there would be two *e*'s. [5]

Rule XXXVI is really covered by the Rule II. The suffix *er*, however, was counted. Table XXVI shows the grade placement and frequency of both the roots and the derivatives. It is interesting to note that the exception is *engineer*.

Rule XXXVII.—A word ending in *y* after a vowel usually retains the *y* before any suffix. [5]

There are twenty derivatives governed by this rule, with eleven root words from which they are derived. There are no excep-

TABLE XXIV

SUMMARY FOR RULE XXXI

Grade	Frequency
Grade 5	4
Grade 6	5
Grade 7	4
Grade 8	9
Total	22

TABLE XXV

GRADE PLACEMENT OF WORDS GOVERNED BY
RULE XXXII

Grade	Frequency
Grade 3	2
Grade 4	5
Total	7

TABLE XXVI

SUMMARY FOR RULE XXXVI

Grade	Roots	Derivatives	Exceptions
Grade 2	2	..	..
Grade 3	2	2	..
Grade 4	1	1	..
Grade 5	2	2	..
Grade 6	2	2	1
Grade 7	1	2	..
Total	10	9	1

tions. The root words are at lower grades than the derived forms.
Table XXVII gives the grade placement and frequency.

Rule XXXVIII.—In adding *ing* to a word ending in *ie*, drop
the final *e* and change *i* to *y*; as *tie, tying.* [5]

There are five words ending in *ie*. These are *die, lie, tie,* and
pie at Grade 3 and *necktie* at Grade 5. At Grade 6 *dying* con-

forms to this rule. At Grade 5 there is *lying* derived from *lie*. Table XXVIII gives the grade placement and frequency.

SUMMARY

Table XXIX is a general summary of the rules. The figures in the first column indicate the rule; the figures in the second column refer to the number of derivatives governed by the rule; the figures in the third column refer to the number of words that are exceptions. In the last two columns are given the grade placement of these derived forms. For example, for Rule I, there are 125 derived words which conform to this rule (plurals in *s* or *es*) and twenty-five exceptions to the rule. About 50 per cent of these derivatives fall below Grade 5 and the greatest number appear in Grade 4. Each rule has been summarized in a similar manner. It will be seen that the number of exceptions for Rule VIII has not been entered. According to the detailed

TABLE XXVII
SUMMARY FOR RULE XXXVII

Grade	Roots	Derivatives
Grade 2	6	1
Grade 3	0	3
Grade 4	1	1
Grade 5	1	6
Grade 6	2	1
Grade 7	1	3
Grade 8	0	5
Total	11	20

TABLE XXVIII
SUMMARY FOR RULE XXXVIII

Grade	Roots	Derivatives
Grade 3	4	0
Grade 4	0	0
Grade 5	1	1
Grade 6	0	1
Total	5	2

TABLE XXIX

SUMMARY OF THE DATA ON THE RULES

Rule	Number Governed by Rule	Number of Exceptions	About 50 Per Cent of the Words Fall Below Grade	Grade of Greatest Frequency
I	125	25	5	4
II	167	4	6	8
III	20	0	4	3–4–5
IV	16	0	6	8
VI	14	0	7	8
VIII	58	?	6	6
IX	131	30	6	6
XI	21	0	7	5–6
XII	2	0	4	3–5
XIV	1	0	..	5
XV	98	28	6	7
XVI	See rule 8	..	..	..
XVII	7	0	8	8
XX	1	0	..	4
XXI	16	1	7	6
XXIII	16	0	6	5
XXIV	54	0	8	8
XXV	12	0	..	5
XXVIII	248	339	5	4
XXIX	..	..	..	..
XXX	..	..	..	..
XXXI	22	2	8	8
XXXII	7	0	..	4
XXXV	..	..	..	..
XXXVI	9	1	8	3–5–6–7
XXXVII	20	0	6	5
XXXVIII	2	0	..	5–6

analysis of this rule, it is hardly possible to determine the number of derivatives or the number of exceptions because of the vague way in which the rule is stated. The number of exceptions is zero, 13, or 25, depending upon the interpretation of the rule.

It will be seen that one or more grades appear in the last column. The reason for this is that the frequency is the same for some derivatives in more than one grade.

Inspection of Table XXIX reveals a number of interesting facts. Rules I, IX, and XV have a high percentage of exceptions, while Rule XXVIII has more exceptions than it has regular derivatives. Thirteen rules have no exceptions. Of these thirteen only Rule XXIV governs more than fifty words, or, to be exact, this rule affects only 1.3 per cent of the entire list. Although these thirteen rules are consistent, their frequency is certainly low.

Inspection of the tables under the individual rules shows that, in general, derivatives are found at higher grade levels than their base words and are, therefore, judged to be harder to spell.

Many of the rules as stated are confusing and are parts of more general rules. For example, Rule XXXVI is part of Rule II. If it seemed necessary to make a specific rule, such as Rule XXXVI, it could include all the suffixes with *e*, such as *ed*, *en*, and *est*. Also, Rules IV and XXI could be combined into one general statement about suffixes beginning with vowels. It will be seen from Table XXIX that if these two were combined, the number of derivatives governed by such a rule would be doubled and yet there would be only one exception. Thirteen of the twenty-seven rules analyzed deal with learning to spell derived words.

Finally, this study of the generalized statement commonly used points to the following conclusions:

1. Some rules would perhaps function much better in written composition or when dictation exercises are used. See Rule XXVII or Rule XXXV.
2. For a rule to be valuable there must be both frequency and consistency, that is, the more words governed by the rule and the fewer the exceptions, the greater the value of the rule.
3. If 30 per cent of the rules have to do with derivatives, as is the case with these rules, perhaps they should be taught after the pupil has mastered most of the words that are in the minimum essential list. If derivatives are harder to spell than the base words, their rules might come later to enable pupils to increase their spelling vocabularies after they have mastered a basic list.

BIBLIOGRAPHY OF SPELLERS

1. ALEXANDER, GEORGIA. *A New Spelling Book*. Longmans, Green and Company, New York, 1922-1928.
2. ARNOLD, SARAH LOUISE. *The Mastery of Words*. Iroquois Publishing Company, Syracuse, N. Y., 1923.

3. BOARD OF EDUCATION. *Course of Study and Syllabus in Spelling for Elementary Grades.* Board of Education, New York City, 1928.
4. BREED, F. S. and FRENCH, W. C. *The Breed-French Speller.* Lyon and Carnahan, New York, 1927.
5. BROWN, M. E., BURDICK, W. H. and JEFFERS, G. B. *The Composition Speller.* Rand McNally and Company, New York, 1928-1930.
6. HORN, E. and ASHBAUGH, E. J. *Lippincott's Horn-Ashbaugh Speller.* J. B. Lippincott Company, Philadelphia, 1920.
7. JONES, W. F. *The Jones Complete Course in Spelling.* Hall and McCreary Company, Chicago, 1924.
8. KALLOM, A. W. and EBY, FREDERICK. *The Star Speller.* Newson and Company, New York and Chicago, 1927.
9. LEONARD, S. A. and WINSHIP, E. A. *The New Merrill Speller.* Charles E. Merrill Company, New York, 1925.
10. LEWIS, E. E. *The Common Word Speller.* Ginn and Company, Boston, 1921.
11. McCALL, W. A. and HOUSER, J. D. *The McCall Speller.* Laidlow Brothers, New York, 1925.
12. PHILLIPS, C. A. and POWELL, M. M. *The Universal Speller.* Houghton Mifflin Company, Boston, 1929.
13. RAMSAY, E. E. and ROW, R. K. *The New National Speller.* Row, Peterson and Company, Chicago, 1926.
14. REEDER, WARD G. *Two Thousand Spelling Demons.* Silver, Burdett and Company, Newark, N. J., 1925.
15. SMITH, J. H. and BAGLEY, W. C. *Mastery Speller.* D. C. Heath and Company, New York, 1929.
16. STARCH, D. and MIRICK, G. A., *The Test and Study Speller.* Silver, Burdett and Company, Newark, N. J., 1928.
17. THORNDIKE, E. L. and WOHLFARTH, J. H. *Growth in Spelling.* World Book Company, Yonkers, N. Y., 1929.
18. TIDYMAN, W. F. *Supervised Study Speller.* World Book Company, Yonkers, N. Y., 1924.
19. TRABUE, M. R. and STEVENS, B. A. *Trabue-Stevens Speller.* Row, Peterson and Company, Chicago, 1929.
20. TROWBRIDGE, C. R. *Constructive Spelling.* The Macmillan Company, New York, 1928.

CHAPTER V

RELATION OF FREQUENCY OF WORD ELEMENTS TO ERRORS IN SPELLING

Types of Errors

The Institute of Educational Research collected the errors made by the children in a typical New York City public school on each of most of the words in the list used in the present study. These misspellings were carefully analyzed and classified into thirty-one classes with subdivisions, following in general the scheme used by Mendenhall [10]. Finally from these thirty-one classes fifteen major types of errors, which included fifty per cent of all errors, were selected in order to get a workable classification which would serve as a basis for diagnostic work in spelling.

The next task was to count the number of words by grades in which these common errors might logically appear. Table XXX shows this count. The types of errors are described in the first column. The actual number of words in each half grade in which such an error could appear is found in the succeeding columns. The last column shows the total for the 4,065 words. Taking, for example, the error described, "Omitting a final e," it is found that there are 39 words ending in e in Grade IIA, 27 in Grade IIB, etc., with a total of 804 words out of the 4,065 which end in final e.

As was shown in Chapter IV, writers of textbooks in spelling have certainly tried to help children generalize on the final e. Still, the most common error found in the study on errors was the adding of a final e to a word or to any syllable of a word. This error appeared 298 times out of a possible 4,091 times and "Omitting the final e" appeared 151 times. Rules on final e either are not being adequately taught or are not functioning.

Inspection of Table XXX reveals that items 1 and 15 have not been counted by grades. It is possible for any consonant

Generalization in Spelling

TABLE XXX

NUMBER OF WORDS BY GRADES THAT WOULD BE MISSPELLED IF CHILDREN MADE EACH OF THE MOST COMMON TYPES OF ERRORS

Error	2A	2B	3A	3B	4A	4B	5A	5B	6A	6B	7A	7B	8A	8B	Total
1. Doubling a consonant															4,065
2. Omitting the second of a double consonant	13	21	21	23	38	33	33	38	48	56	56	53	55	85	573
3. Omitting the second of a double vowel ..	13	15	14	18	17	21	20	17	12	4	6	7	3	9	176
4. Omitting a final *e* ...	39	27	36	33	53	61	63	70	56	82	76	75	61	72	804
5. Omitting a silent letter which is not a final (not counting 4, 6, 10, 13)	2	3	11	7	8	5	9	12	23	12	2	2	2	2	100
6. Omitting the *i* of the phonogram *ai*, as in *nail*	1	4	6	7	9	8	12	10	10	4	8	4	8	3	94
7. Substituting *i* or *ey* for final *y*	17	12	7	20	24	18	31	33	29	30	22	35	43	55	376
8. Omitting the *c* of the phonogram *ck*	1	3	6	6	15	9	6	4	1	6	5	2	2	0	66
9. Transposing final *le*, making it *el*	3	0	1	2	11	5	9	11	9	6	9	14	10	10	109
10. Omitting the *a* of the phonogram *ea*, as in *each*	5	6	16	12	23	17	17	28	12	6	14	8	9	9	182
11. Substituting *k* for hard *c*	9	11	17	4	25	22	23	15	49	60	58	66	103	100	562
12. Substituting *s* for soft *c*	1	2	1	1	3	3	3	3	24	22	19	34	32	49	197
13. Omitting the *e* or the *ed* in words ending in *ed*	1	7	13	24	13	10	7	19	21	23	24	26	32	18	238
14. Interchanging *ie* and *ei*	1	0	7	5	4	7	14	14	16	14	9	11	12	17	131
15. Substituting a vowel for a vowel															4,065

to be doubled or for any vowel to be substituted for any other vowel. The number of errors that could be made would be represented by the sum of all the consonants or all the vowels used in the word list. Further research is needed on the consonants doubled and the vowels substituted most frequently.

In Table XXXI the common errors are given and the number of times they occurred is compared with the total number of times they could occur in the list of words. For example, the first error is "Doubling a consonant." This misspelling appeared in 143 words and could appear in any of the 4,065

TABLE XXXI

NUMBER OF TIMES THE MOST COMMON ERRORS WERE FOUND COMPARED
WITH TOTAL NUMBER OF WORDS IN WHICH SUCH ERRORS COULD
BE MADE

Error	Frequency of Occurrence	Total from Table XXX
1. Doubling a consonant	143	4,065
2. Omitting the second of a double consonant	217	573
3. Omitting the second of a double vowel ...	34	176
4. Omitting a final *e*	151	804
5. Omitting a silent letter which is not a final (not counting 4, 6, 10, 13)	294	100
6. Omitting the *i* of the phonogram *ai*, as in *nail*	36	94
7. Substituting *i* or *ey* for final *y*	33	376
8. Omitting the *c* of the phonogram *ck*	16	66
9. Transposing final *le* making it *el*	19	109
10. Omitting the *a* of the phonogram *ea*, as in *each*	53	182
11. Substituting *k* for hard *c*	11	562
12. Substituting *s* for soft *c*	113	197
13. Omitting the *e* or the *ed* in words ending in *ed*	49	238
14. Interchanging *ie* and *ei*	35	131
15. Substituting a vowel for a vowel	805	4,065

words. The second error is "Omitting the second of a double consonant." There were 217 such misspellings and such an error could occur in only 573 of the words in this list. Attention is called to type error 5, "Omitting a silent letter which is not final." There were 294 such misspellings. As there are only 100 words in which such an error could occur, it would be necessary for two or more such errors to appear in a single word. Type error 15, "Substituting a vowel for a vowel," accounted for 805 words being misspelled out of a possible 4,065.

A comparison of types of errors with the number of words in which it is possible for such errors to occur has much significance. For instance, error 2 is committed in more than one-third of the words having double consonants in the word list. Error 8 appears in roughly one-fourth of the words, while error 12 occurs in over one-half of the words. If Tables XXX and XXXI are studied together, it can be determined in what grades each of these words appears with the greatest frequency.

Summary

A classification of 50 per cent of all errors made in spelling words from the list used in the present study revealed fifteen major types of errors. The word list was analyzed to determine the number of words in which each of these fifteen types of errors could occur.

Tables XXX and XXXI show the number of words actually misspelled and the number that could be misspelled according to the classification, and give their grade distribution.

CHAPTER VI

SUMMARY AND CONCLUSIONS

The purpose of the present study was to make a comprehensive analysis of a carefully selected list of spelling words, with reference to the visual configuration of the words, their phonetic elements, the frequency and consistency with which certain rules can be applied to the spelling of the words, and the frequency of appearance of certain word elements which are commonly misspelled.

The results of this investigation can be summed up briefly in the following points:

1. The visual analysis shows accurately the frequency of appearance of word elements, that is, which word elements are rare, which word elements never appear, and the grade placement of all of the word elements.

2. The phonetic analysis shows the frequency of the word elements, and their consistency or inconsistency of pronunciation.

3. The application of the rules to the word list reveals both the frequency and the degree of consistency of correct spelling by rules, together with the grade level of frequency and exceptions to the use of rules.

4. The frequency of the word elements in which the common errors could be made is determined by grades.

In general, this study points to the following conclusions:

1. Since some letter combinations are much more frequent than others, it would probably be better, other things being equal, to emphasize the most frequent rather than the less frequent visual elements if investigations should show that it is desirable to emphasize any of the visual elements.

2. Since certain letter combinations are pronounced in a larger number of different ways than other letter combinations, it is probably desirable, other things being equal, to teach the child to make the more common and consistent phonetic translations, than to study the less common and the less consistent ones.

3. Since certain letter combinations appear with considerable frequency as the equivalent of each of a number of different sounds, it would seem desirable to conduct further investigations concerning the desirability and methods of teaching the pupil to use phonograms of this type.

4. Since it appears that many rules either apply to very few cases or have a relatively large number of exceptions it is suggested that such rules should be treated with caution until experimental evidence concerning their functional value is secured.

5. Since some of the rules, although they may be applied to many words, are difficult to understand and to apply even by an adult with the aid of a dictionary, it would seem advisable to treat such rules with caution until their functional value in the elementary school is established experimentally.

6. Since a small number of rules are relatively easy to understand and have relatively few or no exceptions, it would appear advisable to use primarily such rules, if any, until the functional value of the more complicated rule or rules with frequent exceptions has been established.

7. Since slight differences in the statement of a rule often result in a different number of cases falling under the rule and a different number of exceptions, it is apparent that the greatest care should be exercised in stating a rule.

8. If a given rule is to be used in a textbook, it is important to know at what grade level it will appear first, at what grade level it will appear most frequently, and where there are the greatest number of exceptions, if any. The data presented show the grade distributions for the rules studied.

9. There is a need of further investigation of the relation between the common errors made in spelling words and the usefulness of rules in preventing these errors. This is desirable for the reason that certain rules apply in many cases to parts of words that are infrequently misspelled, whereas other rules apply chiefly to the parts of the words which are most frequently misspelled.

10. If prefixes, suffixes, contractions, abbreviations, etc., are going to be taught, it is valuable to determine where they appear in relation to the basic words with which they are going to be used, whether at the same, at a lower- or at a higher-grade level.

This study in no way settles the question of generalization.

It aims rather to point out the necessity for the analysis of the individual words which are going to be taught.

Finally, the practical uses of this analysis at the present time are as follows:

1. It serves as part of the basis for diagnostic work in spelling.

2. It provides the data essential for experimental studies of the value of generalization in spelling.

3. It provides material which may be used in psychological investigations of the fundamental characteristics of the process of generalization and transfer of training.

4. It provides data of value in attempting to achieve a "reform" in spelling.

5. It provides data which may justify at once the elimination of certain rules and generalizations now employed in many spelling systems.

6. It enables an investigator to select the rules and generalizations which are of possible value and hence worthy of further study.

7. It provides data that may be employed in the discovery of hitherto unused bases of generalization in spelling.

BIBLIOGRAPHY

1. ARCHER, C. P. "Saving Time in Spelling Instruction." *Journal of Educational Research,* XX (September, 1929), pp. 122-131.

2. BREED, F. S. *How to Teach Spelling.* F. A. Owen, Dansville, N. Y., 1930.

3. CARROLL, H. A. *Generalization of Bright and Dull Children.* Contributions to Education, No. 439. Bureau of Publications, Teachers College, Columbia University, New York, 1930.

4. GATES, ARTHUR I., *The Psychology of Reading and Spelling.* Contributions to Education, No. 129. Bureau of Publications, Teachers College, Columbia University, New York, 1922.

5. GATES, ARTHUR I. and CHASE, ESTHER HEMKE. "Methods and Theories of Learning to Spell Tested by Studies of Deaf Children." *The Journal of Educational Psychology,* XVII (May, 1926), pp. 289-300.

6. GATES, ARTHUR I. *New Methods in Primary Reading.* Bureau of Publications, Teachers College, Columbia University, New York, 1928.

7. HORN, ERNEST. "Principles of Method in Teaching Spelling as Derived from Scientific Investigation." *Eighteenth Yearbook of the National Society for the Study of Education,* Part II. Public School Publishing Company, Bloomington, Ill., 1919, pp. 52-77.

8. HORN, ERNEST. "The Child's Early Experience with the Letter A." *The Journal of Educational Psychology,* XX (March, 1929), pp. 161-168.

9. HORN, ERNEST. "The Influence of Past Experiences upon Spelling." *The Journal of Educational Research,* XX (April, 1929), pp. 283-288.

10. MENDENHALL, J. E. *An Analysis of Spelling Errors.* A Lincoln School Publication. Bureau of Publications, Teachers College, Columbia University, New York, 1930.

11. PRYOR, H. C. and PITTMAN, M. S. *A Guide to the Teaching of Spelling.* The Macmillan Company, New York, 1921.

12. THORNDIKE, E. L. and GATES, A. I. *Elementary Principles of Education.* The Macmillan Company, New York, 1929.

13. THORNDIKE, E. L. "The Need of Fundamental Analysis of Methods of Teaching." *The Elementary School Journal,* XXX (November, 1929), pp. 189-191.

14. TIDYMAN, W. F. *The Teaching of Spelling.* World Book Company, Yonkers, N. Y., 1926.

15. TIDYMAN, W. F. and JOHNSON, EDITH. "Value of Grouping Words According to Similar Difficulties in Spelling." *Journal of Educational Research,* X (November, 1924), pp. 297-301.

16. WAGNER, CHARLES A. *Experimental Study of Grouping by Similarity as a Factor in the Teaching of Spelling.* Doctor's Dissertation, University of Pennsylvania, Philadelphia, 1912.

17. WATSON, ALICE E. *Experimental Studies in the Psychology and Pedagogy of Spelling.* Unpublished Doctor's Dissertation. Teachers College, Columbia University, New York, 1925.

APPENDIX

"A"

Grade 2A

aa	ab	ac	ad	ae	af	ag	ah	ai	aj	ak	al	am
	baby	back	bad		after			said		make	all	am
	table	1	glad		1			1		take	ball	came
	2		had							2	call	name
			made								fall	same
			road								tall	4
			5								5	

Grade 2B

aa	ab	ac	ad	ae	af	ag	ah	ai	aj	ak	al	am
	rabbit	black	bread			ago		chair		brake	snowball	game
	1	face	head			flag		hair		cake	walk	1
		teacher	read			2		rain		wake	2	
		3	reading					train		3		
			4					4				

Grade 3A

aa	ab	ac	ad	ae	af	ag	ah	ai	aj	ak	al	am
	about	each	dead		afraid	again		afraid		makes	alone	cream
	above	place	made		leaf	rag		again		making	called	1
	2	2	reader		2	wagon		air		speak	half	
			ready			3		fair		takes	shall	
			spade					painted		taking	small	
			5					painting		5	steal	
								6			talk	
											talked	
											talking	
											walking	
											wall	
											walls	
											12	

* There is a similar sheet for every letter and for every grade through Grade 8.   The numbers represent

SHEET *

(First Half)

an	ao	ap	aq	ar	as	at	au	av	aw	ax	ay	az
an		apple		are	as	at		gave	away		away	
and		cap		car	ask	cat		have	1		day	
can		papa		dark	fast	eat		2			hay	
hand		3		dear	has	fat					lay	
man				ear	last	gate					play	
ran				far	was	hat					plaything	
6				hard	6	late					say	
				hear		rat					stay	
				warm		sat					today	
				year		that					way	
				10		what					10	
						11						

(Second Half)

an	ao	ap	aq	ar	as	at	au	av	aw	ax	ay	az
any		apples		arm	asked	boat	aunt	having	saw		may	
candy		paper		around	grass	coat	Santa Claus	1	1		pay	
can't		2		bark	wash	father	2				played	
many				bear	washing	pat					says	
pan				star	4	water					Sunday	
sand				yard		5					5	
Santa Claus				6								
stand												
than												
want												
10												

(First Half)

an	ao	ap	aq	ar	as	at	au	av	aw	ax	ay	az
anything				card	Christmas	ate	because	leave	crawl		birthday	
clean				carry	class	hatched	1	leaves	1		yesterday	
hands				cars	east	hate		2			2	
hang				garden	glass	skate						
land				heard	pass	skating						
mean				mark	washed	5						
rang				nearly	6							
sang				part								
8				sharp								
				start								
				tear								
				wear								
				12								

the totals for each grade.

Generalization in Spelling

PHONOGRAM SHEET
ab as in

Grade	(*baby*)		(*rabbit*)		(*about*)	
2A	baby table	2				
2B			rabbit	1		
3A					about above	2
3B						
4A	stable	1	tablet	1		
4B	able	1	absent cabbage grab	3		
5A						
5B	unable	1	cabin	1		
6A	labor	1	habit	1	vegetable	1
6B					abuse	1
7A			absence	1	comfortable favorable miserable probable probably remarkable valuable	7
7B	label	1	absolutely cabinet elaborate taxicab	4	agreeable considerable disagreeable profitable reliable	5
8A	cable	1	abstract establish established Sabbath	4	ability aboard abroad abundant advisable available capable changeable lovable payable uncomfortable	11

PHONOGRAM SHEET (*Continued*)

ab as in

Grade	*(baby)*		*(rabbit)*		*(about)*	
8B	enable	1	absurd		abundance	
			laboratory	2	comfortably	
					considerably	
					desirable	
					honorable	
					liable	
					probability	
					reasonable	
					respectable	
					syllable	10

TOTAL		9		18		37